Mal Great Again: The Truth Will Set You Free

MW01518592

Logan Truehart

Table of Contents

Introduction: The Journey to Wisdom

Do you remember when life made sense? When a dollar actually meant something, jobs were everywhere, and buying a home didn't mean signing your soul over to the bank? It wasn't that long ago. Your parents or grandparents could support a family on one income. Kids could walk to school without a second thought. Hard work paid off, and common sense wasn't a rare skill.

But then, something changed.

The media stopped reporting facts and started spinning stories. Politicians promised everything and delivered nothing. Schools stopped teaching real skills and started pushing nonsense. And little by little, the life that once felt stable and fair started slipping away.

Now, they tell you **this is just the way things are.** That struggling is normal. That inflation just "happens." That you need a degree (and a mountain of debt) just to scrape by. They want you distracted, exhausted, and too busy to ask the only question that really matters:

Who's been lying to us?

I know what it's like to trust the system. I did everything right—worked hard, got a degree, landed a solid job. And yet, I still couldn't afford a home in Vancouver. Thirty years ago? No problem. Today? Forget it. The rules have changed. The game is rigged. And they don't want you to figure that out.

But here's the truth: **You don't have to play along.**

This book isn't here to tell you what to think. It's here to teach you **how to think.** To sharpen your instincts, cut through the noise, and spot the tricks the media, the government, and the elites use to manipulate you.

Because once you see their game for what it is, **you'll never be fooled again.**

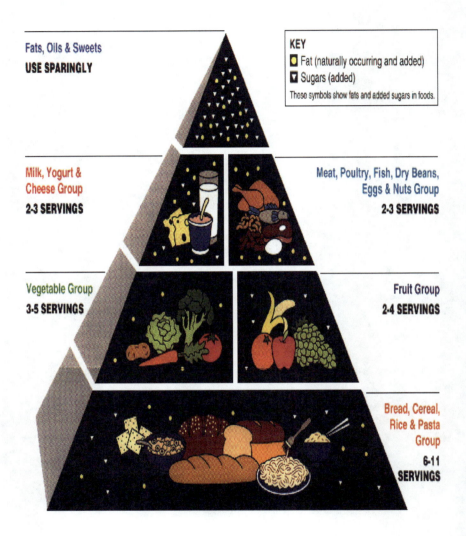

Fats, Oils & Sweets
USE SPARINGLY

KEY
🟡 Fat (naturally occurring and added)
🔻 Sugars (added)
These symbols show fats and added sugars in foods.

Milk, Yogurt &
Cheese Group
2-3 SERVINGS

Meat, Poultry, Fish, Dry Beans,
Eggs & Nuts Group
2-3 SERVINGS

Vegetable Group
3-5 SERVINGS

Fruit Group
2-4 SERVINGS

Bread, Cereal,
Rice & Pasta
Group
**6-11
SERVINGS**

Chapter 1: What Are They Lying About Now?

The Lies: How You've Been Misled

Let's start with a simple fact: **You've been lied to.** Over and over again. By the schools, by the media, by the so-called "experts." They told you things as if they were the absolute truth, and you had no reason to doubt them—until, one day, you started seeing the cracks in the story.

The Food Pyramid Scam

Remember the food pyramid they taught us in school? The one that said bread, cereal, and pasta should be the biggest part of our diet? **Carbs, carbs, and more carbs.** Meanwhile, they told us that fat—steak, butter, eggs—would clog up our arteries and kill us. Turns out, that was **completely wrong.** The real problem? Sugar and processed junk—exactly the stuff they told us was fine in moderation. **Who benefited from that lie?** Big food corporations, selling you cheap, addictive garbage, and Big Pharma, selling you pills after you got sick.

The "Go to College" Trap

How many times did they tell you, **"Go to college, get a degree, and you'll be successful"**? They drilled it into our heads: no degree = no future. So millions took out massive loans, only to find themselves drowning in debt, working jobs that don't even require a degree. Meanwhile, the guys who went into the trades—**plumbers, welders, truckers**—are making six figures with no debt. But they didn't tell us that, did they? Because universities wanted their money, and the banks wanted you **trapped in debt for life.** So much that you cannot declare bankruptcy against student loans in the US.

The Iraq War Lie

How about this one: **"Iraq has weapons of mass destruction."** Remember that? It was the excuse to send our sons and daughters off to war. We spent **trillions of dollars, thousands of lives lost**—and for what? No WMDs were ever found. **It was a lie.** But the politicians who pushed that war? They got richer. The **defense contractors, the oil companies, the elites who never sent their own kids to fight**—they all made a killing while working-class Americans paid the price.

The Great Recession Bailout

And speaking of getting screwed, remember 2008? The housing crash? **Wall Street gambled with people's homes and savings, lost everything—then got bailed out.** The banks got trillions of your tax dollars, while regular Americans lost their homes, their jobs, their pensions. They told us it was about "saving the economy." But who really got saved? The elites. The rich got richer. **You got nothing.**

Inflation: The Hidden Tax

They want you to believe inflation is "natural," that prices always go up. **But why wasn't inflation a huge problem when your grandparents were young?** Because back then, money wasn't being printed like monopoly money. Now, they flood the system with cash, making everything **more expensive while your paycheck stays the same.** Who benefits? The government, the banks, the corporations. Who suffers? **You.**

The list goes on. **They lied about history, about money, about war, and about health.** And every single time, **the same people walked away richer and more powerful, while regular folks paid the price.**

So here's the real question: **If they lied to you before... what are they lying about now?**

Why Do They Want You Uninformed?

It's simple: **An uninformed public is easy to control.** If you don't know the truth, you can be manipulated. You can be made to believe things that aren't real. You can be **scared into submission** or distracted from the real issues.

Think about it:

- If you really understood how the financial system works, would you spend **30 years paying off a mortgage** while the banks get rich off your interest?

- If you knew how politicians on **both sides** actually operate, would you waste your time fighting your neighbor over left vs. right—while the real crooks are laughing **above both of you**?

- If you saw how corporations use **psychological tricks** to make you buy things you don't need, would you still fall for their scams?

They don't want you to **see the bigger picture.** That's why the media keeps you focused on garbage—celebrity drama, viral social media fights, fake scandals. They **want you glued to the screen**, feeding you outrage and fear, because **a scared and angry person is easier to control.**

Meanwhile, politicians **stir up division**—making sure you're too busy arguing about culture wars to notice **how the system is rigged against you.** And the schools? Instead of teaching **real-world skills** like how to manage money, how to think critically, or how to spot propaganda, they push **obedience and memorization.** They don't want thinkers. **They want followers.**

Because here's the truth: **When people are overwhelmed, distracted, and uninformed,**

they're easy to manipulate. They won't question why their lives are getting harder while **the elites keep getting richer.** They won't notice how **every crisis** is used as an excuse to take away more of their freedom. **They'll just accept it and move on.**

But you don't have to play their game.

First Step: Question Everything

If you take **one thing** away from this chapter, let it be this: **Never take anything at face value.**

If the **government** says something—**question it.**
If the **media** says something—**question it.**
If a **billionaire** says something—**question it.**

Ask yourself:

- Who benefits if I believe this?

- Has this source ever lied before?

- What do they want me to feel right now—**fear, anger, outrage?**

- Is there actual proof, or just someone telling me what to think?

- Are they trying to sell me something—an idea, a product, a political agenda?

- Does this information make me feel helpless, or does it empower me?

The moment you start asking these questions, **you take back control.** You stop being an easy target for manipulation. You stop falling for the same tricks **over and over again.**

They **count on you** being too tired, too distracted, too overwhelmed to question them. They **want** you doom-scrolling social media, getting angry at the latest outrage, never stopping to ask:

Who is pulling the strings?

But once you wake up to their game, **you can never go back.** You start seeing the patterns. You start noticing how the same tactics are used **again and again.** And most importantly—**you start thinking for yourself.**

In the next chapter, we'll expose **one of their biggest weapons against you: your emotions.** Because when they control your feelings, **they control your mind.**

Chapter 2: Feelings vs. Facts

How Emotions Are Used to Manipulate You

Ever notice how the news, politicians, and big corporations always seem to be trying to make you **angry** or **scared**? That's not an accident. **It's a trick.** And it's one of the oldest tricks in the book.

Here's why: **When you're emotional, you stop thinking clearly.**

When you're fired up, you don't stop to ask, *"Wait a minute, is this even true?"*

Instead, **you react.**

And that's exactly what they want.

Think about the last time you saw a headline that made your blood boil. Something like:

- **"You Won't Believe What They're Planning Next!"**

- **"The Shocking Truth They Don't Want You to Know!"**

The people writing that stuff **know exactly what they're doing.** They're **pushing your buttons.** Because when you're emotional, **you're easier to control.**

Fear: Their Favorite Weapon

If they can make you scared, **they can make you obey.**

How many times have they told you:

- **"If you don't do this, disaster will strike!"**

- **"This is the biggest threat we've ever faced!"**

- **"You MUST act NOW, or it will be too late!"**

Governments, big media, and even corporations **use fear** to make you go along with whatever they want.

But here's the truth: **If someone is trying to scare you into believing something, it's a red flag.**
Real truth doesn't need fear to sell itself.

Anger: The Ultimate Distraction

Anger works the same way. When they make you mad, **they can control where that anger goes.**

Ever wonder why politicians are always blaming someone else for your problems?

- **"It's the immigrants!"**
- **"It's the trans people!"**
- **"It's those people over there!"**

They do it so **you don't look too closely at them.**

It keeps you distracted.
And it works.

Taking Back Control

So next time you feel yourself getting emotional over something you see on the news or online, **STOP** and ask yourself:

1. **Who benefits from me feeling this way?**

2. **Am I reacting, or am I thinking?**

3. **What are they NOT telling me?**

The moment you start asking those questions, **you take back control.**
You stop being a puppet.
You start thinking for yourself.

And that, my friend, is **the last thing they want.**

Why Headlines Trigger Fear and Anger

Ever wonder why news headlines **never sound calm and reasonable**?

They're always dramatic, extreme, and designed to **hit you right in the gut.**

- **"OUTRAGEOUS: Look What They're Doing Now!"**
- **"SHOCKING: This Will Change Everything!"**
- **"WARNING: You're Not Safe Anymore!"**

It's not just clickbait—it's a psychological trap.

Fear and anger make you click. They make you **engage, share, argue, and keep coming back.**

The media knows this. They're not in the business of informing you.
They're in the business of **getting your attention**—because attention means **money.**

- When you **click**, they make money.
- When you **share**, they get more clicks.
- When you **argue in the comments**, they get even more engagement.

They don't care if what they say is **true, half-true, or completely misleading.**
They care about **making sure you feel something strong enough to keep scrolling.**

Fake Outrage vs. Real Problems

Now ask yourself:

- Why does the media keep pushing **left vs. right**, when both political parties serve the same corporate interests?

- Why do they tell you to **blame other working people**—whether it's immigrants, the poor, or the middle class—while billionaires keep getting richer?

- Why do they stir up **social fights** over race, gender, and culture, but never focus on the real issue: **the people at the top controlling everything**?

Because if they keep you **fighting your neighbors**, you'll never look up and realize **who's actually in charge.**

The **real fight isn't left vs. right.** It's **top vs. bottom.**

The people making the rules—the billionaires, the corporate elite, the career politicians—they don't care what side you're on. **They just want you distracted.**

While we argue over petty issues, **they're the ones writing laws, controlling wealth, and rigging the system** to keep us working harder while they collect more.

Think about it:

- The media tells you to blame the "other side" for economic problems. But who really profits when wages stay low and prices go up?

- They push fear about crime and instability. But who benefits when you feel unsafe and desperate?

- They tell you to hate the "other group," but who walks away with record profits while we fight each other?

The moment you **stop playing their game** and start asking **who's actually benefiting**, the whole illusion falls apart.

The moment you stop reacting emotionally and **start thinking critically,** you'll see the pattern. And once you see the pattern, **you can't unsee it.**

The Danger of Feeling Right

Have you ever read a news story, seen a meme, or heard a political speech and thought:

"That sounds EXACTLY right!"

That's a warning sign.

If something makes you **feel good, justified, or validated**, you're more likely to believe it— **without questioning it.**

And that's **exactly** what manipulators count on.

- **If you already dislike a politician, you'll believe any scandal about them—true or not.**

- **If a post confirms what you already think about the world, you won't stop to check if it's real.**

- **If a news story makes your "side" look good, you'll share it without a second thought.**

This is called **confirmation bias**—and it's one of the biggest ways they control people.

They don't have to convince you.
They just have to tell you what you already want to hear.

How They Use This Against You

The biggest manipulations in history didn't work because they were logical.
They worked because they **felt right** to the people who believed them.

- **The WMDs in Iraq?** People wanted to believe it, so they did.

- **The housing bubble before 2008?** People wanted to believe prices would never go down, so they did.

- **"This time will be different"—before every financial crash?** People wanted to believe it, so they did.

Truth doesn't care how you feel.

So next time you hear something that makes you **immediately nod your head in agreement**, stop.
Ask yourself:

1. **Do I believe this because it's true, or because I want it to be true?**

2. **Where's the proof?**

3. **Who benefits from me believing this?**

Because the second you stop letting **feelings** decide what's true...
You start taking back control of your mind.

Chapter 3: Digging for the Truth

Spotting Fake News

If you've ever clicked on a headline and felt tricked into reading something completely different than what you expected, you've been a victim of **clickbait**. But misleading news is more than just annoying—it's dangerous. It shapes public opinion, fuels outrage, and spreads false narratives that keep people misinformed and divided.

So how do you spot it before it fools you? Here's what to look out for:

1. Sensationalist Headlines

Ever see a headline like:

- *"You Won't Believe What Happens Next!"*

- *"This ONE Thing Will Destroy America as We Know It!"*

- *"The Shocking Truth They Don't Want You to Know!"*

These are designed to **hijack your emotions**—anger, fear, excitement—so you **click without thinking**. When you're emotional, you're less likely to question the content. That's exactly what they want.

Before reacting, ask yourself:

- *Does this headline sound like it's trying to make me angry or scared?*

- *Is it vague and over-the-top instead of giving clear facts?*

- *Does it use words like "shocking," "outrageous," or "exposed" to get a reaction?*

If so, **proceed with caution.** A real news story doesn't need to use cheap tricks to get your attention.

2. Headlines That Don't Match the Actual Story

Sometimes, the headline is technically true—but it leaves out key details to mislead you. This is called **"framing"**—where they present real information in a way that **twists the truth**.

Example:

- **Headline:** *"New Law Will Let Criminals Walk Free Without Jail Time!"*
- **Reality:** The law might only apply to **non-violent offenders** with minor infractions.

The goal? **Make you assume the worst before you even read the article.**

Whenever you see a shocking claim, **read past the headline** and look for the full context.

3. No Clear Sources

Real news stories tell you where they got their information. Fake or misleading news loves to use **vague sources** like:

- *"Experts say..." (Which experts?)*

- *"Sources close to the situation..." (Who?)*

- *"Reports suggest..." (Which reports? Where's the proof?)*

If an article doesn't link to **actual sources**— official reports, direct quotes, or verifiable data —it's a red flag. **They want you to trust them without evidence.** Don't fall for it.

4. Only Showing One Side of the Story

A good news article gives you **both sides** of an issue. A misleading one? It cherry-picks facts to push an agenda.

For example:

- A story about a protest might only show **violent moments**, ignoring peaceful demonstrations.

- A political article might **quote one party heavily** while barely mentioning the other side.

A real journalist asks tough questions—even when it challenges their own beliefs. If an article feels one-sided, **look for another source** that covers the same topic.

5. History of Spreading Misinformation

If you keep seeing misleading or emotionally charged news from the same place, **stop trusting them.** Some outlets exist just to push propaganda, not truth.

Quick ways to check if a source is sketchy:

- **Look up their past stories.** Do they have a habit of exaggerating or getting things wrong?

- **Check if they issue corrections.** Legitimate news sources **admit mistakes.**

- **See who funds them.** Some "independent news" sites are secretly backed by political groups or billionaires with an agenda.

A quick Google search like *"Is [news site] reliable?"* can reveal a lot.

Bottom Line: Think Before You Click

Misleading news thrives because people **share first and think later**. If a headline **makes you emotional**, that's your cue to **pause and fact-check**.

- **If it sounds too outrageous to be true... it probably is.**

- **If it's only giving one side... look for another source.**

- **If it won't tell you where the info came from... don't trust it.**

Stay skeptical. Stay sharp. **And never let anyone do your thinking for you.**

Simple Fact-Checking Techniques Anyone Can Use

Think about how many times you've shared something online just because it *felt* true. Maybe it made you mad, maybe it confirmed what you already believed, maybe it was just too shocking *not* to share. But later, you found out it wasn't quite right—or worse, completely false.

That's how misinformation spreads. It preys on emotion. But here's the good news: stopping it is easier than you think. You don't need a fancy degree or hours of research. A few simple tricks can help you tell truth from lies in seconds.

1. Google It—But Look for More Than One Source

If something sounds too crazy to be true, don't just take it at face value. Type it into a search engine and see what comes up. But here's the trick: don't just trust the first thing you see.

Ask yourself:

- **Are multiple sources reporting the same thing?** If only one sketchy-looking site is making the claim, that's a red flag.

- **Do these sources have different perspectives, or do they all say the exact same thing?** If multiple articles repeat the same sentences, that could mean they all came from one place.

But here's where it gets tricky: **Just because multiple sources exist doesn't mean they're independent.** Many news outlets are owned by the same few companies. If five different sources all belong to the same parent company, they'll likely push the same narrative, no matter what the truth is.

2. Who Owns the News?

It's easy to assume that because different websites are reporting something, it must be true. But a little digging can show you whether those sources are truly independent—or just different brands owned by the same company.

Here's how to check:

- **Search "[News Outlet Name] parent company."** This will tell you who owns it.

- **Go to the bottom of a news website—** sometimes they list their ownership in small print.

- **Check financial filings or Wikipedia.** Major media companies are usually public, so their holdings are documented.

If multiple articles covering the same topic all lead back to the same parent company, that's a sign they might be controlling the narrative.

Real independent verification means checking sources that aren't connected.

3. The Image Tricks

Ever see a picture of a huge crowd at a rally and think, *Wow, that's insane!*—only to find out later it was from ten years ago? That's a classic trick.

A quick way to bust these fakes:

- Right-click the image (or press and hold on your phone) and search where else it's been used before.

- If that same "breaking news" photo was actually taken years ago, you've just caught them lying.

This happens all the time. A photo of a fire gets labeled "Protesters destroying the city *right now!*"—except it's from another country. A picture of empty grocery shelves goes viral with "The economy is collapsing!"—except it's from a storm years ago. Fake news loves old pictures. Don't fall for it.

4. Check the Date

Some stories were true *at some point,* but that doesn't mean they're true *now.*

Example:

- You see a headline: **"Mass Layoffs Hit the Country's Biggest Companies!"**
- You panic—until you check the date and realize the article is from 2008.

This happens a lot. People dig up old news to stir up fear. Always check when something was published before you assume it's current.

Bottom Line: Trust, But Verify

Bad information spreads because people believe first and think later. But **you** don't have to be one of them. Before believing or sharing something:

- **Check if it's coming from multiple independent sources—not just different brands owned by the same company.**

- **Look for proof—actual links, data, or direct quotes.**

- **Ask yourself if it's designed to make you react emotionally before thinking.**

If something holds up to those tests, great. If not? You just outsmarted the people trying to manipulate you. That's real power.

Why Sources Matter

Imagine this: You're at a bar, and some loud guy you've never met before leans over and whispers, *"Hey, did you hear the government is secretly controlling the weather?"*

Would you immediately believe him? Or would you ask, *"Who the hell are you, and where did you hear that?"*

That's how you should treat every piece of information you come across—whether it's on TV, social media, or even from a friend. **Who is saying it, and how do they know?**

A claim is only as good as the source it comes from. If your car breaks down, you don't ask a random guy on the street what's wrong with it— you ask a mechanic. So why trust an anonymous social media post over actual experts when it comes to important issues?

Here's how to separate trustworthy sources from ones that just want to manipulate you.

Trustworthy Info: Trace the Source

The easiest way to spot unreliable information is simple: **It won't tell you where it came from.**

Think about it. If someone is telling the truth, they have no reason to hide their sources. They should be able to back up what they say with hard facts, official records, or real quotes.

Watch out for statements like:

- *"Many people are saying..."* (Who? Name one.)

- *"A recent study shows..."* (Which study? Can I read it myself?)

- *"Insiders report..."* (Which insiders? Are they even real?)

How to check:

- If an article makes a big claim but doesn't link to real sources, be suspicious.

- If a website only links to *itself* or vague "reports," that's another red flag.

- If you Google the claim and only find it on one sketchy-looking site, it's probably false.

Legitimate news sources aren't afraid to tell you exactly where they got their information. Fake news wants you to just trust them blindly.

Who Benefits from You Believing This?

Every piece of information has a purpose. Some is meant to inform you, some is meant to sell you something, and some is meant to control what you think.

Before you trust a source, ask:

- Who benefits if I believe this?

- Is this trying to inform me—or manipulate me?

- Is this coming from someone with an agenda?

For example:

- If a company says, *"This new miracle pill will make you lose 20 pounds in a week!"*—

they're probably just trying to sell you something.

- If a politician says, *"The other side is destroying the country!"*—they probably just want your vote.

- If a media company repeatedly pushes a specific message, check who owns them. Their parent company might have a financial or political interest in making you believe certain things.

Trustworthy information doesn't need to trick you. It gives you the facts and lets you decide for yourself.

Be Skeptical of "Breaking News" and Viral Stories

In today's world, information spreads at the speed of light. The problem? **The first version of a story is often wrong.**

Ever notice how the first reports of a big event always seem chaotic and full of contradictions? That's because **when things are happening fast, nobody has the full story yet.**

The media, social media influencers, and random people on the internet all rush to be the first to say something—whether it's true or not.

Before you get outraged, ask yourself:

- Is this story brand new? If so, wait a bit—more details will come out.

- Is everyone rushing to conclusions without proof? If yes, be skeptical.

- Are people using this event to push a political agenda before the facts are clear? That's a huge red flag.

Misinformation spreads fastest when people react emotionally instead of thinking critically. **Don't be manipulated—wait for real facts to come out.**

The Too-Good-to-Be-True Test

Some stories sound way too perfect—like they were custom-made to confirm exactly what you already believe.

If a headline makes you think, *"Wow! This proves I was right all along!"*—stop and fact-check.

Why? Because fake news thrives on giving people **what they want to hear** instead of what's actually true.

Think about it. If someone really wanted to trick you, wouldn't they feed you the exact kind of story that fits your beliefs perfectly?

Good journalism isn't about making you feel good—it's about telling you the truth, even when it's inconvenient. If a story seems too perfect, too extreme, or too outrageous, double-check before you believe it.

Consider Opposing Views

Let's be honest: Nobody likes hearing the other side of an argument. It's uncomfortable. But if you only listen to sources that tell you what you want to hear, you're **not learning—you're being programmed.**

Ask yourself:

- Am I only getting my news from sources that already agree with me?

- Have I ever actually listened to a different perspective with an open mind?

- If this story was about someone I support, would I still believe it?

Strong thinkers **seek out opposing views** not because they agree with them, but because they want to challenge their own thinking.

You don't have to change your mind—but if you refuse to even hear another side, you're no longer thinking for yourself.

Check Who Owns the Sources You're Relying On

A common mistake people make is thinking they're getting news from different sources when, in reality, **they're all owned by the same parent company.**

A handful of massive corporations own the majority of news networks, websites, and newspapers. This means that even if you check multiple sources, you might still be getting the same narrative from the same people behind the scenes.

How to check:

- Look up the name of the news source and see who owns it.

- If multiple sources all trace back to the same parent company, that's not independent verification—it's the same message being repeated.

- If a company or government owns a news outlet, be especially critical of their coverage on issues that affect them.

Real independent sources don't all say the exact same thing. If every outlet is pushing the same story in the exact same way, it's worth asking why.

Bottom Line: Be a Detective, Not a Puppet

Anyone can learn how to spot bad information. You don't need a fancy degree, and you don't have to trust anyone blindly. You just need to **ask the right questions:**

- Who is saying this, and how do they know?
- Can I verify this claim from multiple independent sources?
- Does this source have a reason to lie or manipulate me?

- Is this information designed to make me react emotionally before thinking?

- Have I checked if the story is being reported differently by others?

The people who control information want you to be passive, emotional, and easy to manipulate. **The moment you start questioning everything, they lose their power over you.**

Think for yourself. Demand proof. Never let anyone do your thinking for you.

Chapter 4: Who's Controlling the Narrative?

Ever get the feeling that the news, social media, and even entertainment are all pushing the same ideas at the same time—like they're reading from the same script? That's not an accident.

The people in power—whether they're billion-dollar corporations, career politicians, or media elites—want to control what you think. Not because they care about the truth, but because **your beliefs shape your actions.** And if they control your actions, they control **everything.**

Think about it:

- **What you see determines what you believe.**
- **What you believe determines how you vote, what you buy, and who you trust.**

- **If they control what you see, they control what you do.**

The Hidden Hands Controlling Information

You might think you have access to a wide variety of opinions, but in reality, **most of the media, social networks, and even fact-checkers are owned by a handful of massive corporations.**

These companies aren't run by neutral truth-seekers. They're run by executives with financial and political interests. And when **a few powerful people** control **what stories get told, how they're framed, and which ones get buried**, they can shape entire nations.

How?

- **News companies decide which stories get covered—and which get ignored.** If a scandal threatens their interests, it might disappear before you even hear about it.

- **Tech companies control what you see online.** Their algorithms boost what they want you to believe and bury what they don't. If they don't like your opinion, they can silence it completely.

- **Entertainment is loaded with messaging.** Whether it's Hollywood, music, or TV, there's always a subtle (or not-so-subtle) push toward certain narratives.

You don't even have to censor people when you can **manipulate what information reaches them in the first place.** That's the real game.

Why Would They Lie?

The biggest mistake people make is assuming that powerful people always tell the truth. But ask yourself—what benefits them more?

Telling you the truth? Or making you believe whatever helps their agenda?

The truth often exposes corruption, bad policies, or the lies they've told before. But if they can **keep you distracted, divided, or chasing the wrong enemy,** you'll never notice what's really going on.

They push certain stories over and over because:

- **They need you to believe their version of events.**

- **They want you to support the policies that benefit them.**

- **They want you to hate who they tell you to hate—so you never turn your anger toward them.**

This isn't conspiracy—it's basic power dynamics. The more they control what people believe, the easier it is to keep power.

How to See Through the Illusion

If you want to break free from their control, you have to **stop taking information at face value** and start **questioning why you're being told something in the first place.**

- **Look at who owns the source.** Is this an independent voice, or is it controlled by a major corporation or government?

- **Follow the money.** Who benefits if you believe this? Are they selling you something? Do they gain power if you're afraid?

- **Ask what they** *aren't* **telling you.** If all the major outlets are covering the same thing at the same time, what's being ignored?

Once you start seeing the patterns, you'll realize that **the game isn't about truth—it's about control.** And the only way to win is to think for yourself.

Why Both Sides Get Manipulated

If you think only the "other side" is being lied to, manipulated, and brainwashed—think again. **Both sides get played.** The left, the right, and everyone in between.

Why? Because **division is a tool.** And the people in power use it to keep everyone distracted while they continue to call the shots behind the scenes.

The Divide-and-Conquer Strategy

Throughout history, leaders have used one simple trick to stay in power: **keep the people fighting each other so they never unite against the real problem.**

If you're busy blaming the other side, you'll never stop to ask:

- **Who benefits from this constant division?**

- **Why are they always fueling outrage instead of solutions?**

- **What would happen if we stopped fighting each other and focused on them?**

They don't want you to think that way. They want you angry, emotional, and too distracted to see what's really going on.

How They Manipulate Both Sides

No matter where you fall on the political spectrum, you've been targeted. **Every group gets their own customized version of manipulation.**

- **If you lean right:** They'll feed you stories designed to make you fear losing your country, your culture, or your freedoms. They'll tell you the left wants to destroy everything you love, so you'll fight them instead of questioning the people actually making the rules.

- **If you lean left:** They'll bombard you with messages about injustice, inequality, and threats to democracy—convincing you that the right is out to take away your rights, so you'll never look at the elites running the system behind the scenes.

Both sides are **fed half-truths, cherry-picked facts, and emotionally charged stories** designed to **keep them hating each other.**

And while you're busy fighting over politics, guess what?

- The same powerful corporations keep making billions.

- The same corrupt politicians stay in office.

- The same broken system keeps running exactly the way they want it to.

The Illusion of Choice

You're told you have two choices: Left or Right. But what if that's **the biggest lie of all?**

- What if the system isn't as black and white as they make it seem?

- What if both parties serve the same interests at the top?

- What if the biggest issues—corporate corruption, government overreach, media control—never get solved *because both sides benefit from keeping them in place?*

The truth is, **real power isn't held by Democrats or Republicans, liberals or conservatives—it's held by the people behind the scenes who pull the strings on** *both.*

How to Break Free from the Left-vs-Right Trap

If you want to truly think for yourself, you have to **step outside the narrative they've built for you.**

- **Stop assuming "your side" is always right.** Every group gets manipulated. Nobody is immune.

- **Recognize when they're using emotion to control you.** If a story makes you instantly angry or afraid, ask why they want you to feel that way.

- **Look at who's really benefiting.** If a politician or media outlet is stoking division, what do they gain from it?

- **Focus on solutions, not just outrage.** They want you stuck in endless arguments. The real power is in seeing the bigger picture and demanding real change.

The moment you stop letting them control how you see the world, **you become impossible to manipulate.** And that's what they fear the most.

How Independent Thinking Empowers You

If you've ever felt powerless—like no matter what you do, the system stays broken, the rich get richer, and the same corrupt people stay in charge—there's a reason for that. **They've convinced you that you don't have power.**

But here's the truth: **You have more power than they want you to believe.** And it starts with independent thinking.

Why They Fear Independent Thinkers

The people running the show—big corporations, politicians, media moguls—they **don't** want a nation of people who think for themselves. That would ruin the whole game.

What they want instead:

- People who react emotionally without questioning the source.

- People who fight each other instead of holding the powerful accountable.

- People who repeat talking points instead of asking real questions.

- People who feel too small and helpless to challenge the system.

When you start thinking for yourself, **you break free from their control.**

- You stop falling for their emotional manipulation.

- You stop letting them decide what you believe.

- You stop being just another pawn in their game.

What It Means to Think Independently

Independent thinking isn't about being a rebel for the sake of it. It's about **choosing your own**

path instead of letting someone else program your mind.

That means:

- **Questioning everything—even what you already believe.** Nobody is right 100% of the time. Stay open to new information.

- **Doing your own research.** Not just clicking the first search result—**really digging** into sources, motives, and biases.

- **Watching for manipulation tactics.** Whenever a story tries to make you *feel* instead of *think*, step back and ask *why*.

- **Not letting others tell you who your enemy is.** The real enemy is the one keeping you distracted and divided.

The Power of a Free Mind

A person who thinks for themselves is a person who can't be controlled. That's why independent thinking is the ultimate power move.

When enough people wake up to how they're being played, the entire system of manipulation **falls apart.**

- The media loses its grip.

- Politicians can't win by using fear and division.

- Corporations can't distract you from their corruption.

And suddenly, **real change becomes possible.**

The world doesn't change because politicians pass new laws. **It changes when people stop being blind followers and start thinking for themselves.**

They don't want that. But you should.

Chapter 5: Spotting the Tricks—Propaganda 101

How Repetition Makes Lies Feel Like Truth

Have you ever noticed how a lie repeated over and over can start to feel like an undeniable fact? It's no coincidence. Just as that catchy tune burrows into your head until you can't stop humming it, the same message played on loop can alter your beliefs. Our minds crave **familiarity**, and when a message is repeated, it eventually becomes part of what we consider "common sense."

Consider one of the most striking examples: the engagement ring. For decades, advertising campaigns have hammered home the idea that an engagement ring should cost **two months' worth of your paycheck**. They've convinced millions that this is the only way to show love and commitment. But here's the cold, hard truth —diamonds are not the rare treasures they're made out to be. In reality, diamonds are **abundant and relatively inexpensive**.

The diamond industry, backed by a near-monopoly, controls the market by **artificially limiting supply** and **repeating the same message**: "You must spend two months' salary on a ring." This tactic doesn't just build an emotional connection; it **manipulates pricing**. When you look at the numbers, the markups are staggering. While the actual cost of mining and processing a diamond might only be a fraction of the retail price, profit margins can soar beyond **300%**. That means for every dollar spent on production, you could be paying three dollars or more at the register.

Think about it:
   • **Why do you believe that spending two months' salary on a ring is normal?**
   • **Who benefits when the price is inflated by hundreds of percent?**

- **What real evidence supports the idea that diamonds are inherently valuable?**

When a message is repeated enough—like the idea that diamonds are rare and priceless—it transforms into "truth" in your mind, even if it's built on manipulation. Every time you hear that engagement rings should cost a certain amount, your natural skepticism is slowly worn away by the power of repetition. They want you to forget to question the **monopoly tactics** and the inflated numbers that serve only to **enrich the few** at the expense of the many.

So, the next time you see that slogan or hear that repeated claim, **stop and ask yourself:**
- **Who truly benefits from me believing this?**
- **Are these numbers based on real value, or are they engineered to exploit my emotions and trust?**
- **Am I thinking for myself, or merely accepting a message that's been drilled into me over and over again?**

Every time you let **repetition** replace critical thinking, you lose a bit of your **freedom**. Don't let your mind be programmed by marketing that thrives on emotional manipulation and inflated promises. **Stand up for your worth** and reclaim your power to see through the lies. Your ability to think independently is your greatest strength—protect it against the noise of repeated deception.

Why Certain Voices Are Silenced

History teaches us that controlling information is a powerful tool. Consider how, during one of the darkest chapters of the 20th century, regimes used ruthless censorship to crush dissent—tactics that echo in the past with figures like **Hitler**, who carefully controlled what the public could read and hear. In a similar vein, modern governments such as those in North Korea and Russia employ strict controls over media and online content to shape public opinion and silence challenging voices.

Today, while the context has changed, the underlying techniques remain remarkably similar. There are instances where **social media platforms** have, at times, moderated content in ways that favor a certain narrative. Without pointing fingers too directly, some have noted that recent changes in leadership at major tech companies have coincided with increased scrutiny over posts and discussions—leading to questions about whether all viewpoints are getting a fair hearing.

Likewise, there are mild indications that some political figures have taken steps to restrict the expression of protest on university campuses, a move that echoes past methods of **information control**. These actions, though presented in subtler terms today, share a common purpose: to keep dissenting voices from challenging the dominant narrative.

Ask yourself:

- **Who benefits when only one version of the story is allowed to flourish?**
- **What might be lost when diverse opinions are pushed aside?**
- **Are we missing out on important perspectives because of a pattern of silencing?**

By recognizing these echoes from history—whether in the blatant censorship of the past or in the more nuanced methods of today—we reclaim our power to think independently. Don't let any force, past or present, decide what you can or cannot hear. Your **independent thought** is essential to a free society, and it deserves to be heard in full.

How Emotional Manipulation Keeps the Masses Distracted

Emotions are a powerful force—one that can distract you from the truth and keep you from questioning the status quo. When fear, anger, or joy overwhelm you, there's little room left for critical thinking. That's why many in power know exactly how to play on your emotions. They create stories and images designed not to inform you, but to make you feel something intense, whether it's **panic**, **outrage**, or even misplaced **happiness**.

Think about how dramatic news headlines, designed to shock you, can leave you reeling. A barrage of alarming messages makes you focus on the emotion, not on the details. Soon, you're busy reacting—sharing posts, arguing in the comments—while the real issues slip by unnoticed. It's a clever tactic: by **amplifying emotion**, they ensure you remain distracted from the facts that matter.

Consider these examples:

• **Fear-mongering reports** about distant threats keep you on edge, even if the danger is minimal.

• **Overblown stories** about economic collapse

or social unrest can stir up anger and despair, diverting your attention from systemic issues.

• **Heartwarming viral videos** and feel-good stories, though pleasant, can also be used to drown out hard truths and critical debate.

Every time you let your emotions take over, you risk losing sight of reason. **Emotional manipulation** turns your reactions into a tool that reinforces the dominant narrative—one that benefits those in control. So when you feel overwhelmed by strong emotions, **pause**. Ask yourself:

• **What am I really reacting to?**

• **Is this emotional response clouding my judgment?**

• **Am I missing a bigger picture because I'm caught up in the moment?**

By recognizing the power of emotion and learning to step back, you can reclaim your **clarity** and **critical thinking**. Don't let emotional manipulation keep you distracted. Stay alert, question what stokes your feelings, and let your independent thought be your guide in a world designed to keep you busy with distractions.

Chapter 6: The Power of Asking 'Why?'

Why Curiosity is the Ultimate Weapon Against Deception

Curiosity is the mind's armor against manipulation. The moment you stop asking questions, you start accepting whatever you're told. And in today's world—where every headline, every ad, every politician, and every so-called "expert" is trying to sell you a version of reality—**blind acceptance is a recipe for disaster.**

Think about it. **Why do scams work?** Why do politicians get away with blatant lies? Why does the media push narratives that fall apart with the slightest bit of scrutiny? **Because people don't ask questions.** They take things at face value. They assume that if something sounds official, it must be true. But that's how they control you. That's how they get away with it. **They count on your silence.**

But curiosity? **Curiosity breaks the spell.** It's the antidote to deception. A single "Why?" can unravel an entire illusion. That's why the powerful hate people who think for themselves. That's why the media demonizes anyone who questions the official story. The last thing they want is a nation of critical thinkers. **They need obedient followers, not independent minds.**

Curiosity forces you to dig deeper. It makes you seek out the truth instead of just swallowing what's served to you. It turns you into a detective, not a puppet. Instead of reacting emotionally to what you hear, you start investigating. You ask:

- **Who benefits from me believing this?**

- **Where's the evidence?**

- **What aren't they telling me?**

And once you start asking these questions, something amazing happens—**you become**

immune to their tricks. The manipulations, the propaganda, the emotional baiting—it all starts to fall apart. You begin to see the patterns, the contradictions, the outright lies. And once you see them, you can't unsee them.

That's why curiosity is so dangerous to those in power. **A nation that asks questions is a nation they can't control.** They rely on your passivity. They want you too distracted, too overwhelmed, or too scared to question them. But once you refuse to take things at face value, their grip on you weakens.

So let me ask you—**when was the last time you questioned something you were told?** When was the last time you dug deeper instead of just accepting the narrative? Because if you're not questioning, **you're being controlled.** It's that simple.

Real-Life Examples of System Challengers

History doesn't remember the obedient. It remembers the **troublemakers, the rebels, the ones who refused to swallow the lies.** These are the people who saw through the deception, stood their ground, and **proved the system wrong.** And guess what? The system **hated** them for it.

1. The Whistleblower Who Exposed Government Lies

In the early 1970s, a man named **Daniel Ellsberg** did something unthinkable—he leaked a top-secret government report, the **Pentagon Papers,** exposing how the U.S. government had been lying about the Vietnam War for years. The media, politicians, and military leaders had all played along, feeding the American people a false narrative. But Ellsberg had the courage to **question the official story** and take action. The government called him a traitor. They tried to destroy him. But the truth was out, and public opinion shifted. **One man's curiosity shattered a government deception.**

2. The Scientists Who Refused to Bow to "Consensus"

Ever heard of **Ignaz Semmelweis?** Probably not. But he saved millions of lives—and was mocked, ridiculed, and dismissed by the so-called "experts" of his time. In the 1800s, doctors had no concept of germs. They would go from performing autopsies straight to delivering babies—without washing their hands. Mothers and newborns were dying in droves. Semmelweis saw the pattern, started asking questions, and realized **washing hands could save lives.** The medical establishment laughed at him. They called him a lunatic. They destroyed his career. But guess what? **He was right.** Years later, germ theory proved everything he said. **The so-called "consensus" was dead wrong.**

3. The Journalists Who Took Down a President

Watergate. In 1972, two reporters, **Bob Woodward and Carl Bernstein,** started digging into a simple burglary at the Democratic National Committee headquarters. What they uncovered was **the biggest political scandal in American history.** The White House, the FBI, the CIA—all of them were involved in covering up illegal activities tied to President Richard Nixon's reelection campaign. The government called it a **conspiracy theory.** The media tried to downplay it. Nixon himself denied everything. But Woodward and Bernstein didn't stop. They followed the money, connected the dots, and exposed the truth. **In the end, the most powerful man in the world was forced to resign.** And it all started with two guys who **refused to take the official story at face value.**

What These Stories Teach Us

These people had one thing in common: **they questioned the system when everyone else just obeyed.** They refused to accept the "official story." And when they pulled on that first thread of doubt, **the entire narrative unraveled.**

And here's the thing—**you have that same power.** The ability to challenge lies, to dig deeper, to think for yourself. But you have to **choose** to use it. The system will tell you to shut up. To sit down. To trust the "experts." But if history teaches us anything, it's this: **the so-called experts are wrong all the time.** And the people who change the world are the ones who **dare to ask questions.**

Start Questioning and Thinking Critically

By now, you see the pattern. **The people who change the world aren't the ones who blindly obey—they're the ones who ask questions.** They challenge authority, push back against the narrative, and refuse to be spoon-fed lies.

But here's the good news: **you don't need to be a journalist, a scientist, or a whistleblower to do this.** You just need to start thinking for yourself—**right now.**

Step 1: Ask "Who Benefits?"

Whenever you hear a news story, a government policy, or even a corporate ad campaign, stop and ask: **Who benefits from me believing this?**

- A politician tells you something? **They want your vote.**

- A pharmaceutical company says their product is "safe and effective"? **They want your money.**

- A news outlet pushes a certain agenda? **They want control over how you think.**

This doesn't mean everything they say is false. But it **does** mean you should be skeptical. Follow the money. **Ask yourself: Who has something to gain from me believing this?**

Step 2: Verify Before You Trust

It's easy to see one news clip, a viral tweet, or a flashy headline and think you know the full story. **You don't.** The media takes things out of context all the time. Politicians manipulate data to fit their agenda. Social media spreads **half-truths like wildfire.**

Before you accept something as fact, **verify it.**

- Look at **multiple** sources. If everyone is saying the same thing with the exact same wording, **it's a script.**

- Read the **original** study, law, or document instead of just what the media says about it.

- Pay attention to **what's being left out.** Sometimes the biggest deception isn't a lie —it's an omission.

Step 3: Don't Be a Gullible Contrarian

Here's where a lot of people go off the rails. They realize they've been lied to, and they **swing too far in the other direction.**

- The government lies? **That doesn't mean every single thing is a lie.**

- The media distorts the truth? **That doesn't mean every news story is fake.**

- Big Pharma pushes bad drugs? **That doesn't mean all medicine is poison.**

Some people can fall so deep into "questioning everything" that they stop believing anything. **They reject basic facts. They get sucked into ridiculous conspiracy theories. They become paranoid and unhinged.**

Don't be that guy.

There's a balance. **Critical thinking means questioning things, not rejecting reality.** Use logic, evidence, and reason. **Not everything is a conspiracy—but enough things are that you should stay sharp.**

Step 4: Trust Yourself, Not the Narrative

At the end of the day, **you are responsible for your own mind.** The government isn't going to think for you. The media sure as hell won't. The schools, the corporations, the "experts"—**they all have their own agendas.**

But you? **You have the power to see through it all.**

Stay curious. Stay skeptical. **Ask the hard questions.** And most importantly—**never let anyone do your thinking for you.**

Chapter 7: Becoming a Free Thinker—Your Next Steps

Exercises to Spot Deception

It's easy to think you're too smart to be fooled. **You're not.** No one is. The best manipulators don't make you feel like you're being lied to— they make you feel like **you're discovering the truth.**

This is why you need to **train your mind** to spot deception **before it sinks in.** The world is filled with psychological traps designed to control what you believe, how you feel, and ultimately, what you do. The good news? **You don't have to fall for them.** Here's how to fight back.

Exercise #1: The "Spot the Manipulation" Challenge

Every day, find a **news article, political speech, or ad** and analyze it using this question:

What emotion are they trying to trigger?

Manipulators want you to feel, not think. The stronger the emotional reaction, the easier it is to push an agenda. Look for these red-flag words:

FEAR Words: Catastrophic, crisis, dangerous, unprecedented, deadly, existential threat, war on [X], epidemic, alarming.
Why? Fear makes you easier to control. If you're scared, you'll accept solutions you'd never agree to otherwise.

ANGER Words: Outrageous, shocking, betrayal, extremist, disgraceful, weaponized, corrupt, abuse of power.
Why? Anger makes you take sides without thinking. If they can make you furious, you'll ignore facts that don't fit the narrative.

GUILT Words: Privileged, problematic, complicit, insensitive, reparations, historical injustice, do better.

Why? Guilt makes you easier to manipulate. If they convince you you're part of the problem, you'll submit to **their** solution.

HOPE Words: Revolutionary, once-in-a-lifetime, transformational, progress, unity, "for the greater good."

Why? Hope can be just as manipulative as fear. If they make you think they're leading you toward a **"better future,"** you'll stop questioning where they're actually taking you.

Drill: Take a news article or social media post and highlight the emotion-triggering words. **Ask yourself: If I strip away these loaded words, what's actually left?**

Exercise #2: The 180-Degree Test

Take a statement being pushed by the media or government, and **flip it.** If the opposite sounds absurd, the original statement is **probably manipulative.**

Example: "Censorship is necessary to protect democracy."
Flip it: "Free speech is dangerous to democracy."
See how ridiculous that sounds? That's how you know the original statement is propaganda.

Example: "Disinformation must be stopped to keep people safe."
Flip it: "People are too stupid to think for themselves, so we must control what they read."
Would people accept it if it were worded like this? No? Then it's deception.

Drill: Try this with news headlines. **If the opposite sounds insane, the original is probably manipulative.**

Exercise #3: The "Who Benefits?" Investigation

Every time you hear a new **fact, policy, or narrative**, ask yourself: **Who benefits if I believe this?**

Follow the Money

One of the easiest ways to expose manipulation is to find out **who is profiting from the message.** If a government or corporation is pushing a certain belief, **look at their financial ties.**

- **Example:** A pharmaceutical company says their new drug is a "miracle cure."
  How to check: Look up their stock price after the announcement. Did it skyrocket? Search for lawsuits or whistleblowers speaking against them.

- **Example:** A media company is pushing climate panic nonstop.
  How to check: Research who funds them.

Do they receive government grants or money from green energy companies?

- **Example:** A politician warns about a national security threat.
  How to check: Are defense contractors about to get a massive new contract? Are weapons manufacturers funding their campaign?

Search terms to use:

- "[Company name] political donations"

- "[Organization] funding sources"

- "[Issue] biggest investors"

- "[Policy] lobbying efforts"

Follow the Power

Money is just one side of the equation—**power is the other.** If a new law, policy, or idea makes it easier for the government, big tech, or elites to **control people,** assume there's an agenda.

- **Example:** The government tells you there's a **new crisis** and they need **emergency**

powers to deal with it.
How to check: Research past "temporary emergency powers." Did they ever give them back? (Hint: They almost never do.)

- **Example:** Social media companies ban "misinformation" to keep people "safe."
How to check: Who decides what's misinformation? Why do bans always seem to favor one political side?

- **Example:** A movement suddenly explodes in popularity overnight.
How to check: Does it have corporate sponsorship? Who is funding it? Organic grassroots movements don't get billion-dollar ad campaigns.

Search terms to use:

- "[Law name] government overreach"

- "History of [policy] abuse of power"

- "Who is behind [movement name]?"

- "Leaked emails [organization or policy]"

Drill: The next time you see a viral news story, stop. **Instead of reacting, trace it back.** Who is pushing it? Who gains? What's the real agenda?

How To Fact-Check Quickly

Most people don't fact-check anything. They read a headline, react emotionally, and move on. **Don't be like most people.**

That doesn't mean you need to spend hours digging through obscure sources every time you hear something. **You just need a system.** Here's how to fact-check news and social media quickly and effectively—**without falling into the trap of over-researching and wasting your time.**

1. Check the Original Source (Not Just the Headline)

Headlines are designed to **manipulate, not inform.** They're crafted to **trigger an emotion** —anger, fear, outrage—before you even read the article.

Many people don't read past the headline. The media knows this, so they often word headlines in a way that leads you to believe something **more extreme or misleading** than what the actual article says.

How to check quickly:

- Look for **quotation marks.** If a headline says, "Experts Say the Economy Will Collapse," who are these "experts"? If there are no names, it's likely manipulation.

- **Find the original quote.** If someone is being quoted, search for their full statement. Many times, **media will twist words or remove context.**

- **Reverse the claim.** If the headline says, "Politician X is under fire for corruption," ask: **Who is saying this?** If it's just political opponents, it might be exaggerated.

Example: A headline reads, "Study Shows Climate Change Will Make Earth Unlivable by 2050."

- If you can't find the actual study, that's a red flag.

- Many times, studies are misrepresented. Look for the actual research paper, not just what a journalist says about it.

- Search for "**criticism of [study name]**" or "**peer review of [study name]**."

2. Watch for Weasel Words That Hide the Truth

Certain words allow journalists to **lie without technically lying.** When you see them, your **BS detector should go off immediately.**

Red Flag Words:

- **"Experts say"** → Who are these experts? Are they biased?

- **"Sources close to X report that..."** → Anonymous sources? Could be made up.

- **"Many believe..."** → How many? Five people on Twitter?

- **"Critics argue..."** → Critics from where? The opposing political party?

- **"Could," "might," "potentially"** → Translation: This hasn't happened, but we want you to believe it will.

Example: A news article says, "Some scientists suggest that eating meat could shorten your lifespan."

- Translation: **There's no real proof, but we want you to believe this.**

A good test is to **remove all weasel words** from an article and see if it still says anything meaningful. If the key claims disappear, it was all fluff.

3. Quick Reverse Image Search (Spot AI Images)

If you see a **shocking** photo on social media, **assume it's fake until proven real.**

A quick way to check is to **do a reverse image search:**

- **On a computer:** Right-click the image and select "Search image with Google."

- **On a phone:** Hold your finger on the image and select "Search with Google Lens."

- **Use TinEye.com** for an alternative search.

If the same image appears in older news stories but with a different caption, it's being used deceptively.

How to Spot AI-Generated Images

AI-generated images are becoming more common in fake news, deepfakes, and social media manipulation. Here are some ways to tell if an image is AI-generated:

1. **Check the hands and fingers.** AI struggles with realistic hands, often generating

extra fingers, missing fingers, or distorted hands.

2. **Look at the text in the image.** AI has trouble making readable words or signs in the background.

3. **Examine symmetry and lighting.** AI images often have **unnatural symmetry** or **inconsistent lighting/shadows.**

4. **Look for facial distortions.** AI struggles with **ear symmetry, teeth alignment, and random artifacts** in faces.

5. **Use AI-detection tools.** Sites like "Is It AI?" or "AI or Not" can analyze images and give you a probability of whether they are AI-generated.

4. Cross-Check Headlines Across Different Sources

If a story is true, you should find **the same core facts** across multiple sources.

How to check quickly:

- Search for the **same story on different political sides.** If CNN and Fox News both report it the same way, **it's probably true.** If their versions sound like two different realities, **someone is lying.**

- Look for **neutral sources.** Wire services like **Reuters, AP News, or your local newspaper** often provide less biased summaries.

- **Watch out for disappearing news.** If a major story suddenly vanishes from headlines, **someone powerful doesn't want you to see it.**

5. Don't Trust "Fact-Check" Sites Blindly

Many "fact-checking" sites are just **opinion blogs disguised as neutral sources.**

How to check:

- Search for "**bias in [fact-check site]**" before trusting them.

- See if they **only "debunk" one political side.**

- Some fact-checkers **use misleading tricks,** like rating a true statement "misleading" because they don't like how it was framed.

If a fact-check site **admits the claim is true but says it "lacks context" or "oversimplifies,"** read between the lines. They are often just **reframing the truth to fit a narrative.**

The Bottom Line: Think First, React Later

Fact-checking **doesn't have to take hours.** If you apply these simple strategies, you can **instantly recognize red flags and spot deception.**

Your goal isn't to "debunk" everything. Your goal is to **stop being easily manipulated.** Take two minutes before believing a story, check the basics, and **always ask yourself: Who benefits from me believing this?**

How to Wake Up Loved Ones

Once you start seeing through the lies, it's only natural to want to **shout it from the rooftops.** You want to protect the people you love. You want them to open their eyes, just like you did.

But here's the hard truth:
If you come at people too hard, too fast — they'll shut you out.
They won't listen. Not because you're wrong, but because they feel attacked.

Most people don't want to believe they've been lied to. It's scary. It shakes their entire world. And if you're not careful, your good intentions can **push them even deeper into the illusion.**

This section is about **how to help them wake up — without pushing them away.**

1. Don't Attack. Ask.

Nobody likes being told they're wrong. Nobody wants to feel stupid. So don't lead with confrontation. **Lead with curiosity.**
Ask questions that make people think — not feel cornered.

Instead of saying:

- "That's fake news."

- "You're brainwashed."

- "You actually believe that garbage?"

Try asking:

- **"Why do you think they never cover the other side of this?"**

- **"Did you notice how every station uses the same words? Doesn't that seem odd?"**

- **"Have you ever looked into who funds this organization?"**

You're not trying to win an argument. **You're planting a seed.** Give it time to grow.

2. Regulate *Your* Emotions First

Let's be honest — it's frustrating.
Watching someone fall for obvious lies, especially someone you love, can make your blood boil.

But if you show up with anger, sarcasm, or judgment, they'll feel attacked. **And when people feel attacked, they stop listening.**

Before you speak, take a breath. Ask yourself:

- Am I trying to win... or am I trying to help?

- Is my tone calm and respectful?

- Am I reacting with emotion, or responding with purpose?

Ground yourself. Take a walk. Count to ten. Remind yourself that waking up is a *process.* You had to go through it, too.

The calmer and more curious you are, **the more trustworthy you become.** That's what opens doors.

3. Use Their Own Experiences

People trust what they've lived through. So if someone remembers an event, scandal, or lie they saw with their own eyes, use that. Tie the present to the past.

For example:

- **"Remember when they said [X historical event] was one thing, and years later it turned out to be the opposite?"**

- **"You lived through the [name an old political scandal]. Does any of this feel familiar to you now?"**

This helps them connect the dots — *without you needing to push them.*

And don't underestimate the power of stories. Sharing how *you* woke up, what clicked for you, and how it made you feel, helps them relate without feeling judged.

4. Know When to Step Back

Sometimes, no matter what you say, **they're not ready.** And that's okay.

If someone gets angry, dismissive, or shuts down — don't escalate. **Don't try to "win."** You're not battling *them,* you're battling the lies they've been fed their whole lives.

Just say:

- **"It's okay, I used to believe that too."**

- **"I'm not trying to argue — just sharing what I've seen."**

Then move on. Let it sit. **Your calm, respectful approach will stay with them — long after the conversation ends.** When the truth finally starts cracking their shell, they'll remember that you were patient. And that matters.

5. Be the Example They Can Trust

At the end of the day, your life speaks louder than your words. If you're grounded, confident, kind, and thoughtful — **people will notice.**
And when the world starts to crumble around them, they'll come to you.

You don't need to shove red pills down anyone's throat.
Just be the light. Ask the right questions. Stay steady.
Let them come to their own conclusions — with your gentle guidance.

Final Word

Waking up is not an instant switch. It's a slow burn.
It can take weeks, months, even years. But every seed you plant — every calm, thoughtful question — **brings people one step closer to the truth.**

Don't give up. Don't lash out.

Lead with love. Speak with strength. And always remember: the truth doesn't need to be shouted — it just needs to be heard.

You're doing the work. One mind at a time.

Conclusion: The Truth Will Set You Free

You made it.

If you've come this far, it means something inside you has already changed. **You see the world differently now.**

You understand how deception works. You know how to question, how to think, how to spot the tactics used to manipulate you. And most importantly—**you know that the fight for truth never ends.**

This is not where your journey stops. **This is where it begins.**

Call to Action: Keep Thinking

The world is not going to get any easier. The lies won't stop. The manipulation won't stop. **But now, neither will you.**

From this day forward, **no headline will slip past your radar unchecked.** No emotional buzzword will trick you into blind outrage. No authority will get away with saying, "Just trust us," without you asking, "Why?"

That is power.

Not the power they want you to have—the real kind. **The kind that makes you unbreakable.**

Because here's the truth:

- **A thinking man cannot be controlled.**
- **A questioning woman cannot be manipulated.**
- **A free mind is the most dangerous weapon against deception.**

And now, **you have that weapon.**

Use it. Every day.

When you read the news, ask yourself: *Who benefits?*

When you hear a politician speak, watch *how* they say things, not just *what* they say.

When the media screams for your outrage, pause and ask: *Why do they want me emotional instead of rational?*

Every question makes you stronger. Every lie you see through brings you closer to freedom.

This is how you win. **This is how we all win.**

It's Okay to Not Have All the Answers

Let's get one thing straight—**you don't have to know everything.** No one does. And anyone who acts like they do? **They're lying.**

The truth is a never-ending journey. **Not a destination.**

You will **never** wake up one day and say, "Now I understand **everything** and can never be fooled again." That's not how thinking works. That's not how life works.

And that's okay.

Because **what matters isn't knowing everything—it's refusing to stop searching.**

The moment you decide, *I already know it all—* that's the moment you become just as blind as the people who believe every word the media feeds them. **Arrogance is just another form of ignorance.**

So **stay humble, but stay relentless.**

- **If something doesn't make sense—dig deeper.**

- **If a new fact challenges what you believe—test it, don't reject it.**

- **If you realize you were wrong—admit it, correct it, and move forward.**

That's real strength. **Not clinging to old beliefs —but having the courage to change when the truth demands it.**

This is what separates **real thinkers from blind followers.**

And you? **You're a thinker now.**

Final Words of Encouragement in Misinformation

The world isn't going to change overnight. **Lies will still be spread. People will still be manipulated.** The battle for truth is an endless one.

But now, you see the game.

You see the distractions, the emotional traps, the carefully crafted stories designed to keep people angry, afraid, and obedient.

And now that you see them, **they can't control you.**

That alone makes you stronger than 99% of people.

But strength isn't just about seeing through the lies. It's about **staying sane while doing it.**

Because the truth is, **this path can be lonely.**

- You will meet resistance.

- Some people will call you crazy.

- Some will refuse to listen—because thinking for themselves is too much work.

That's okay.

You don't need to convince everyone.
You just need to keep questioning, keep learning, and **keep thinking.**

Because **truth doesn't need an army. It just needs people brave enough to seek it.**

And you? **You're one of those people now.**

Never forget that.

**SUPPORT
THE CAUSE**

Manufactured by Amazon.ca
Bolton, ON